THE MIDDLE AGES AND PHILOSOPHY

THE MIDDLE AGES AND PHILOSOPHY

On the Ambivalence of Modern Scholasticism

Anton C. Pegis

Delivered as the First James Roosevelt Bayley Lecture

Seton Hall University, 1955

CLUNY
Providence, Rhode Island

Cluny Media edition, 2020

This Cluny edition is a republication of the 1963 Henry Regnery Co. edition of *The Middle Ages and Philosophy*.

....

For this Cluny edition, citation and reference styles have been updated and developed, as needed, for the purposes of clarity and accessibility.

For more information regarding this title or any other Cluny Media publication, please write to info@clunymedia.com, or to Cluny Media, P.O. Box 1664, Providence, RI 02901

VISIT US ONLINE AT WWW.CLUNYMEDIA.COM

ISBN: 978-1950970711

Nihil Obstat: Armand A. Maurer, C.S.B., *Censor Librorum*
Imprimatur: Francis V. Allen, *Auxiliary Bishop of Toronto*
June 20, 1962

Cover design by Clarke & Clarke
Cover image: Jusepe de Ribera, *Aristotle*, 1637, oil on canvas
Courtesy of Wikimedia Commons

CONTENTS

To Gerard Smith, S.J.

whose friendship has been a steady light

PREFACE

IF IT HAS DONE NOTHING ELSE in the last hundred years, scholastic philosophy has strenuously proclaimed and defended its modernity and its right to the prefix *neo-*. Did not the young Mercier proclaim that Thomism should live in the modern world as a neo-Thomism, exposed to the modern sciences, their methods and their progress? Did he not urge it both to modernize itself and to let its claim to authenticity as a philosophy stand on merit? And did not Catholics and non-Catholics alike, with some notable exceptions, agree at the end of the nineteenth century that the merit was not wanting?

During the very decades in which scholasticism has remained unshaken in its ambition to be a pure and rigorous philosophy founded on reason, however, the medieval philosophy which was supposed to have been the source of this ideal has undergone a remarkable and disturbing transformation in the evolution of historical opinion from DeWulf's first history, written in 1895, to Gilson's latest history, written in 1955. Contrary to earlier views, it is held today that there was no self-contained and common medieval scholastic synthesis from which modern scholasticism could have derived its conception of itself as a philosophy living methodically in separation from theology. There was no self-contained philosophy in St. Thomas himself from which a philosophical Thomism might have taken its origin. The great thinkers of the Middle Ages were all theologians, and each one developed his own philosophical ideas as an integral part of his theology. This is a noteworthy result, which throws a curious light on modern scholasticism.

Many, if not most, modern scholastics have been distinctly embarrassed by the notion of "Christian philosophy" on the ground that, like any other authentic philosophy, scholasticism was the work of reason pure and simple. How could it be anything but rational and natural in its substance, respecting the guidance of theology but still free to manage its own house? How, then, could it be *Christian*? But here are historians saying that, however this may be, medieval scholasticism was not a philosophical synthesis, and it did not even have a philosophical existence: it was born within theology, not as philosophy, but as a theological instrument engaged in a supernatural ministry. No doubt, St. Thomas knew very well how to distinguish between theology and philosophy, and he has even taught us the same distinction; but he himself observed the distinction, not to build a philosophy outside his theology, but to use that philosophy in a proper way in order to build a theology. The problem for modern scholasticism lies here, namely, in a theology that includes philosophy, not as an autonomously constituted discipline, but as a theologically employed rational tool.

Those of us who have looked for a philosophy in the *Summa Theologiae* (*ST*) and the *Summa Contra Gentiles* (*SCG*) have somehow found it in works that are essentially theologies. Here we have experienced a dilemma. Wishing to take out of these *Summae* the parts that have seemed to us to be philosophical, we have applied to St. Thomas' theology the distinction that he himself made in his commentary on the *De Trinitate* of Boethius (q. 2, a. 3), namely, that "philosophy is founded on the natural light of reason" whereas "Sacred Teaching is founded on the light of faith." What is more natural, after all, than to distinguish these two lights, in keeping with St. Thomas' own specifications, and to consider as philosophical in both *Summae* whatever is susceptible of being grounded on reason? The principle would certainly work without any difficulty if the *Summae* were mixtures of philosophy. and theology according to the matter treated by St. Thomas; it would even be completely successful if the remarkable idea that the first three books of the *Summa Contra Gentiles* were intended by St. Thomas as philosophy were true. But is it so certain that the principle can be applied to works that are essentially theologies, in which the philosophical materials themselves, being shaped by the light and the purpose that guide the theologian, become thereby theology? Is it certain, in other words, that we can successfully extract philosophy from theology by using the light of reason as our guide and rationality as our yardstick?

The question at issue is not how to build a new philosophy in the proper way; the question is rather the character of St. Thomas' theology and the status of philosophical ideas within it. If, in fact, the theology of St. Thomas includes as integral parts of itself truths that are likewise capable of falling within the scope of philosophy, then we are face to face with a *theological* presentation of truths that the human reason is competent to know. This is the situation before us. St. Thomas, who knew the nature of philosophy, but was not himself a philosopher, created a theology that contained within its supernatural unity not only all that had been revealed but also, in principle, all that the human sciences could teach. The philosophy that we find in the two *Summae* is there at work under the gaze and the direction of the theologian; it is there because, in the name of human salvation, the theologian wants it there as his rational instrument among men. As part of theology, philosophy contains more than its own nature. It contains the theologian's guiding light, and the imprint of his interest and purpose. For this reason, the philosophy in the *Summae* has a dual aspect, namely, its own nature and the divine ministry within which it is living and in whose light it is engaged in a divine work.

The more we think of St. Thomas as a theologian, therefore, and particularly of his philosophy as being theologically engaged, the more we are driven to ask ourselves a simple question. How are we to learn philosophy from St. Thomas? Can we derive philosophy from the two *Summae* by a simple appeal to the light of reason? Such an appeal may tell us what is rational, but if, in the theology of St. Thomas, it be true that rationality can fall on both sides of the distinction between philosophy and theology, how will it distinguish philosophy from theology? And if in the *Summae* rationality is engaged in a divine work, and is there subject to all the privileges of its engagement, how will the light of reason distinguish between philosophy and its ministry, between reason and its engagement, or how will it safeguard the student of St. Thomas from mistaking a separated fragment of theology for philosophy?

The proposition, therefore, that St. Thomas was a theologian and not a philosopher, however much he may have entered philosophy, extends to his theology as well as to the theologian. As works of theology, the two *Summae* have an economy which includes a whole world of philosophical truths under the perspective of revelation: they are there in view of human salvation, and, as there, they are theology. It is this economy in the Thomistic theology that we are beginning to recapture—the economy of the word of God using all the resources of rationality to enable men to open their minds to the truth. Born within such an economy, and dedicated to its service, the philosophy of the *Summae* of St. Thomas was concerned entirely with its religious mission; it was not concerned with the establishment of the demonstrable truths of reason in an independent world of their own. In the presence of such a philosophy, or rather of a philosophy so engaged, the modern Thomist has evidently something to relearn. In spite of dreaming of an autonomous philosophy in the world of today, in spite of thinking that whatever is philosophically demonstrable is formally philosophy, he must learn, against the grain of modern habits, how to read philosophy in the *Summae* as theology in order not to misread it as philosophy.

The present work is a modest and entirely preliminary approach to this very large question. I have tried to see medieval philosophy, and especially the philosophy of St. Thomas, in the world of theology where it was born and lived out its life. I have tried to remind myself that even in St. Thomas' philosophical discussions within the two *Summae*, and this applies in a special way to the first three books of the *Summae Contra Gentiles*, there is present the theological vision and aim of their author. The present-day Thomist will not achieve his own philosophical aim in the modern world until he comes to terms with the theology of St. Thomas in its unity and on its own ground. Except by violent excision, he will not be able to distinguish the philosophy in St. Thomas from his theology until he sees it within its own theological world and with the perspective and imprint of that world.

It is a pleasure for me to thank the President of Seton Hall University, the Most Reverend John J. Dougherty, and the Dean of the College of Arts and Sciences, the Reverend Albert B. Hakim, for inviting me to give the first Bayley Lecture on Founders Day, March 8, 1962, and for their many kindnesses toward me. I wish also to express my gratitude to the Reverend Gerard Smith, S.J., of Marquette University, for generously accepting the dedication of the present lecture.

Anton C. Pegis

Toronto

December 24, 1962

CHAPTER ONE

The Dilemma of Modern Scholasticism

I

The Catholic student of philosophy who has been educated in the scholastic tradition must come sooner or later to stand before an inescapable and difficult problem. He must try to understand a phenomenon called "Catholic philosophy," a body of ideas and principles taught to men and women in Catholic colleges and universities and, apart from seminaries, nowhere else. To be sure, that Catholic schools should wish to teach their own philosophy, and even to develop its virtualities in all domains and levels of education, might seem to be a perfectly normal aim to pursue. What other philosophy should they follow, and what is a philosophy for if not to be carried out?

But "Catholic philosophy" is a peculiar reality if only because of its isolation in the modern world. On the whole, it is perfectly fair to say not only that non-Catholic schools do not accept it, but also, and worse still, that they do not really consider it to be a philosophy. Whatever their choice of adjectives, the prevailing view among them is that a dogmatic believer is an impossibility in the world of philosophy. The mind of such a believer is committed by faith to an order of truths held to be divinely revealed; and because he believes, he is not free to seek truth openly and without preconception or commitment. But how can a committed reason philosophize if, of its very nature, philosophy is a free and open inquiry? How, consequently, can a Catholic school really be teaching a genuine philosophy?

The answer of Catholic schools is well-known. Distinguishing between the specifying objects of faith and reason, they argue that the realm of faith is truly a world of belief in which the Christian is committed to the revealed word of God. The believing Christian lives by and in the light of revelation, a light that is infinitely higher than his own, and he accepts the living Church as his religious teacher. On the other hand, the realm of reason is truly a world of knowledge in which the Christian is not committed to any truths that do not—or cannot—pass the inspection and understanding of human reflection. The Christian as philosopher thus can live—certainly in philosophy—by his own intellectual light, and he can judge truth by means of evidence that he is competent to grasp.

In this way, the Christian walks by both belief and knowledge, both faith and reason; and if, by virtue of its divine certainty, faith seems more excellent to the Christian than does reason, this is a situation that does not demean or undermine rational knowledge, it only points to the supremely higher strength of revealed truth. As a matter of principle, the Catholic as philosopher does not ask his unbelieving colleague to accept his own beliefs as part of philosophy; rather, he asks the unbeliever to accept the reason of the Catholic as an authentic reason in philosophy and the philosophy of the Catholic as a genuine work of reason. From this point of view, Catholic schools feel that they are teaching a philosophy with which non-Catholics of all sorts are certainly free to disagree, but whose legitimacy they should not contest. The fact that Catholic schools are religious schools, teaching a theology that takes precedence over their philosophy, does not mean that they have a less authentic philosophy than do other schools, but that they have the guidance of revealed truth as well. Founded on the natural light of reason, committed even to the proposition that the divine revelation will never deny any truth of philosophy, how can the philosophy taught in Catholic schools not be philosophy in the full and unqualified sense of the term? On what other foundation does a proper philosophy rest? And what other commitment from the side of faith does a philosophy need in order to maintain its own integrity? If theology is founded on faith, however much it uses reason, and if philosophy is founded on reason, however much it is open to the influence of faith, why are not Catholic theology and philosophy both distinct and genuine orders of knowledge, each according to its kind? Why, to limit ourselves to philosophy, is not "Catholic philosophy" or "scholastic philosophy" a perfectly understandable and coherent discipline?

There are good reasons why this conclusion can profitably be re-examined today. Modern scholasticism *does* contain a dilemma within itself, and one need not agree with its opponents or its proponents in order to see this fact. As a philosophy living in harmony with Catholic theology and in communion with what is commonly called "medieval philosophy," modern scholasticism has an intellectual and historical character that could not but be an anomaly in the eyes of some and a peculiar treasure in the eyes of others. To see scholasticism as anything less than an unusual phenomenon is to denature it. To ask how it can be an authentic and coherent philosophy, a genuine work of intellectual reflection, is to point to what is unusual within it: it is a theologically inspired philosophy whose claim to authenticity as a philosophy in no way denies this inspiration. Therein lies, precisely, the dilemma it poses. For its opponents to condemn it for this reason alone may be as premature as it is unwarranted; but for its proponents not to know and acknowledge in full the peculiar nature of modern scholasticism, or (what is much worse) to maintain its internal substance as a philosophy but modify its external shape to enforce its respectability, is a futile and disastrous answer to a serious dilemma.

If, in fact, modern scholasticism—the philosophical movement that has been developing with greater and greater momentum since the middle of the nineteenth century—is a genuine philosophy, why is it so different in scope, in doctrinal content and in method from the prevailing non-scholastic philosophies of the day? Why is modern scholasticism limited almost entirely to Catholics, among whom, as is well-known, it is not free of criticism or opposition? Why, moreover, is modern scholasticism so astonishingly in accord with Catholic theology? This harmony distinguishes scholasticism from non-scholastic philosophies, whether non-Catholic or Catholic, both in fact and in principle. Why are there so many truths of Catholic theology, about God, creation, man, freedom, morality and knowledge expounded and proved in scholastic philosophy and, on the whole, in none other? Indeed, why is scholasticism not only in harmony with Catholic theology but also its doctrinal shadow, very often following its language and its teaching with literal faithfulness? Is scholasticism, then, a philosophy or a theology?

If it is not theology, if it is founded on reason and theology does no more than keep it from error, why is it so full of truths from theology and why is it (and for this very reason) not a commonly acknowledged or recognized philosophy? To be sure, the possession of truth should not bar a philosophy from any earthly philosophical kingdom, but the same possession, being such a unique philosophical phenomenon, cannot but raise a question throughout the kingdom of philosophy. The modern scholastic may not always appreciate the questions of his critics, particularly those critics who see no point in waiting for an answer. Even so, while maintaining the validity of his philosophy, he cannot but recognize his own philosophical isolation, nor can he fail to acknowledge that there is a problem here to engage his attention in a special way.

When we make an effort to see modern scholasticism as we have described it largely through the eyes of its critics, we find that there are, apart from a specific body of doctrines, three characteristic marks in its distinctive attitude as a philosophy. It is modern, it is autonomous, it is Christian. It is open to the modern world of knowledge and to the advances of all the sciences. It is rational in its conduct as a philosophy and, in relation to theology, independent in the natural establishment of its own principles. As an independent rational edifice, it is also in harmony with theology because revelation and reason derive ultimately from the same God; moreover, as distinct from theology by its very nature, philosophy is kept from error by the religious light of theology, which however does not interfere with the internal establishment of philosophical notions themselves. Thus understood, modern scholasticism can claim to be a respectable modern philosophy; it can claim to be a *neo*-scholastic philosophy, just as it can deny that it is some sort of medieval mummy passing as a living reality.

There are deep historical reasons for this strenuous defense of modern scholasticism as a respectable and living philosophy. The scholastic movement in the modern world is not a very old one; indeed, in any significant way it is not very much older than the encyclical *Aeterni Patris* of Pope Leo XIII, issued by that great pontiff on August 4, 1879. Those who are inclined to trace modern Thomism, for example, to the teaching of St. Thomas Aquinas in the thirteenth century may find no trouble in thinking of it as having been transmitted to the modern world more or less in the form in which we know it today. And, no doubt, since the writings of St. Thomas Aquinas have always been available for the modern world to read, it can be argued that his teachings have themselves been readily accessible to the modern student. Unfortunately, philosophical ideas can be lost in history, just as they can be recovered or rediscovered. In this sense, the thought of St. Thomas Aquinas, as well as that of his medieval contemporaries, had almost entirely vanished from Europe by the end of the eighteenth century, and it was slowly being rediscovered by the cooperative work of many scholars during the last decades of the nineteenth century and the first three decades of the twentieth. We who were students in the twenties and the thirties had before us established lines of contact with the world of medieval scholasticism and as a result we did not always realize how little of this medieval theological and philosophical world was known and appreciated by scholastics themselves as late as the middle of the nineteenth century.

If I am here emphasizing the comparatively recent character of modern scholasticism, my reason is to call attention to a fact that may throw some light on scholasticism as a philosophy in our own day. The first scholastic movement in the modern world died of eclecticism before the French Revolution. Descartes and Wolff did not kill it, though they tried. It died because, as a philosophy, it lost its way in the modern world and forgot the sense of its own metaphysical beginnings. The *Philosophia Lugdunensis*, printed in 1782 at the instigation of the Archbishop of Lyons, reveals how little a scholastic manual of that time remembered and retained of the medieval doctrines which it yet sought to present to the modern world; by the same token, this scholastic manual also reveals how many and diverse modern philosophical doctrines it could innocently incorporate within itself.[1] If scholasticism

1. The copy of the *Philosophia Lugdunensis* available in the Institute library is one of the many reprints of this much-read work: *Institutiones Philosophicae auctoritate D. D. Archiepiscopi Lugdunensis ad usum scholarum suae dioecesis editae*, 6 vols.

were to live again in Europe after the French Revolution, it had to be literally recreated. When Leo called the Catholic world to return to medieval scholasticism, and especially to the doctrine of St. Thomas Aquinas, he was therefore giving both an impetus and a direction to a very young movement. Perhaps the most dramatic step was taken by Pope Leo in 1880 when he asked the University of Louvain to establish a chair of Thomistic philosophy. Its first occupant proved to be a man who was at the time a young professor of philosophy in the seminary of Malines, Desiré Mercier, the zealous priest whose forceful personality was to imprint itself on the scholastic

---

in two (Bassani: Typis Remondinianis, 1831). The prefatory letter of the Archbishop of Lyons, Count A. de Malvin de Montazet, dated August 16, 1782, is an interesting historical document (text I, iii-xiv).

On the state of Catholic philosophy after the French Revolution, and especially the beginnings of modern Thomism or scholasticism, see in general: A. Masnovo, *Il Neo-Tomismo in Italia* (Milano: Società Editrice "Vita e Pensiero," 1923); W. M. Horton, *The Philosophy of the Abbé Bautain* (New York: The New York University Press, 1926), pp. 3–55; A. Gemelli, "Neoscolastica," *Enciclopedia Italiana*, Vol. 24 (1934, reprinted, 1949), pp. 581–582; P. Dezza, *Alle Origine del Neotomismo* (Milano: Fratelli Bocca, 1940); ibid., *I Neotomisti Italiani del XIX Secolo*, documents, 2 vols. (Milano: Fratelli Bocca, 1940–1942); A. Walz, "'l Tomismo dal 1800 al 1879," *Angelicum*, Vol. 20 (1943), pp. 300–326; E. Hocedez, *Histoire de la théologie au XIXe siècle*, 3 vols. (Paris: Desclée de Brouwer, 1947–1952); L. Foucher, *La philosophie catholique au XIXe siècle avant la renaissance thomiste et dans son rapport avec elle, 1800–1880* (Paris: Librairie Philosophique J. Vrin, 1955); P. Dezza and G. Santinello, "Neo-scolastica e Neotomismo," *Enciclopedia Filosofica*, Vol. 3 (1957), coll. 874–880; also: J. Bellamy, *La théologie catholique au XIXe siècle* (Paris: G. Beauchesne et Cie., Editeurs, 1904); R. Aubert, *Le pontificat de Pie IX* (Paris: Bloud et Gay, 1952), chs. 4, 6, 8, 9; K. S. Latourette, *Christianity in a Revolutionary Age*, Vol. 1: *The Nineteenth Century in Europe: Background and Roman Catholic Phase* (New York: Harper & Brothers, 1959).

movement of his day from the moment he inaugurated his lectures on modern Thomism in 1882.[2]

This young priest, destined to become the famous Cardinal Mercier, is an excellent example of the character and the aims of scholastic philosophy as it sought to establish itself in the modern world some eighty years ago. The aim and purpose of the young Mercier was quite clear, and his personal response was astonishingly single-minded and forceful. Deeply troubled by the isolation of Catholics within the world of modern scholarship and modern science, and recognizing the harm that the Church had suffered from the prejudice that faith and science were opposed to one another, he set himself the twofold objective of proclaiming the authenticity of modern Thomism as a philosophy and of urging his fellow Thomists to face the task of adjusting their Thomism to the world of modern science and especially to the expansion and diversification of modern

2. On the career of Cardinal Mercier, see the most useful book of L. De Raeymaeker, *Le Cardinal Mercier et l'Institut Supérieur de Philosophie de Louvain* (Louvain: Publications Universitaries de Louvain, 1952), pp. 7–175, 231–246. A number of Cardinal Mercier's papers on philosophy have been edited and brought together by Léon Noël in *Le Christianisme dans la Vie Moderne. Pages Choisies de S. E. le Cardinal Mercier* (Paris: Perrin et Cie, 1919), pp. 31–135. Useful in this connection is the concluding chapter of Mercier's *Les Origines de la Psychologie Moderne*, 2nd ed. (Louvain: Institut Supérieur, 1908), pp. 435–475. On the spirit of Cardinal Mercier, see also L. De Raeymaeker, "Verité et libre recherche scientifique selon le Cardinal Mercier," *Liberté et Verité,* Contributions de Professeurs de L'Université Catholique de Louvain à l'étude du thème proposé a l'occasion du Bicentenaire de Columbia University (Louvain: Publications Universitaries de Louvain, 1954), pp. 13–37.

scientific knowledge. This is how Mercier understood Pope Leo's injunction to the Catholic world to return to St. Thomas.[3] It was a return that involved modernizing Thomism by as much as the task at hand was to create a philosophy that was everywhere the harmonious complement of the sciences. That is why, when he inaugurated his own chair of Thomistic philosophy, Mercier did not hesitate to proclaim as the two pillars of Thomistic philosophy "the union of reason and Christian faith" and "the union of observation and rational speculation."[4] The ideal of the twofold harmony of faith and reason and of reason and the sciences could not be put more succinctly.

This aim, perfectly natural though it may seem, involved scholasticism in general, and Thomism in particular, in a strenuous effort to live as a modern philosophy at precisely the time when it had still to discover in any appreciable way its medieval origins. Today, some eighty years later, we are in a position to see this fact with considerable perspective. Were it not for the zeal of men such as Mercier perhaps we would not uphold so easily the ideal of an autonomous philosophy, a philosophy that aimed to be philosophy and not a hidden defense of faith, a philosophy that was Christian, not by the

3. See, especially, Cardinal Mercier's paper "La philosophie Néo-Scolastique," *Revue Néo-Scolastique*, Vol. 1 (1894), pp. 5–18.

4. The relevant passages of the text of Mercier's 1882 inaugural lecture are quoted in L. De Raeymaeker, *Le Cardinal Mercier*, pp. 49–50.

extrinsic addition of the adjective, but by its intrinsic truth as tested in the marketplace of modern knowledge. Come what may, let us recognize this ideal as a permanent aspect of modern scholasticism. In the hands of Mercier, Thomism was reborn as a radically free philosophy, as engaged in the modern world as any other, seeking both to be informed by the sciences and to bring metaphysical light to them. If this ideal of a free and open philosophy suffered from anything it was from an ignorance of its own history and especially of the historical conditions under which it was created by its founders, the schoolmen of the thirteenth and fourteenth centuries. And this ignorance, seen in the light of present-day notions of medieval philosophy, goes very far. The scholastics of eighty years ago proclaimed the independence of philosophy in the presence of theology in order to maintain its authenticity as a work of the human reason. Today, historians are telling us not only that medieval philosophy, being the creation of theologians, was born in medieval theology, but also that this origin in theology gave to scholasticism its most distinctive intellectual character and formation. Thus, in the transition from 1882 to 1962 we come to stand before the true and lasting paradox of scholasticism as a philosophy, namely, its relations to the Christian revelation and to the medieval theological world in which it was born.

CHAPTER TWO

Medieval Philosophy and Its Historians

II

Taken as a whole, what we call "medieval philosophy" has gone through a considerable evolution in the general appreciation of its historians during the last hundred years.[1] There are at least three stages in this evolution, and we now seem on the point of entering a fourth. What I am here calling a fourth stage is in reality no more than the aftermath of the views expressed by the most distinguished living historian of medieval philosophy, Étienne Gilson. Let me enter my problem by way of the concluding pages of his *History of Christian Philosophy in the Middle Ages.*[2]

Reflecting on the long doctrinal history of Europe that he had followed from the second century to the end of the fifteenth, Gilson found it natural to think over the two distinct influences that were at work in this history, namely, Greek philosophy and Christianity. He noticed in particular that "every time educated Christians came into contact with Greek philosophical sources, there was a blossoming of theological and philosophical speculation."[3] Moreover, recognizing with other historians what he called "the philosophical sterility of ancient Rome,"[4] Gilson stressed the idea that "practically every notable event in the history of Western thought in the Middle Ages is tied up with the presence of a man who had studied in Greece, or who knew Greek and had translated some Greek philosophical writings, or who had access to such translations."[5] The Latin translation of Plotinus early in the fourth century, of Aristotle's *Organon* in the fifth, of the Pseudo- Dionysius in the ninth, and especially of Aristotle's major philosophical writings in the twelfth century, had an enormous effect on the growth and development of Latin Christian speculative thought; so much so, that, "seen from this point of view, the

1. As an outline of such an account one may consult Fernand Van Steenberghen, "L'interpretation de la pensée médiévale au cours du siècle écoulé," *Revue philosophique de Louvain*, Vol. 49 (February 1951), pp. 108–119; "Maurice De Wulf, historien de la philosophie médiévale (1867–1947)," *Revue philosophique de Louvain*, Vol. 46 (November 1948), pp. 421–447; "Réflexions sur les recherches de la philosophie médiévale," *Miscellanea Historica Alberti de Meyer* (Louvain: Bibliothèque de l'Université, 1946), pp. 485–492. Representing a radically different point of view is the essay of Étienne Gilson, "Historical Research and the Future of Scholasticism," *The Modern Schoolman*, Vol. 29, No. 1 (November, 1951), 1–10. See, below, note 14.
2. É. Gilson, *History of Christian Philosophy in the Middle Ages* (New York: Random House, 1955).
3. Ibid., p. 540.
4. Ibid., p. 541.
5. Ibid.

philosophical speculation of the Middle Ages appears as a sort of appendix to the history of Greek philosophy."[6]

But there is another side to the medieval philosophical story and Gilson's name is inseparably related to it. Greek philosophy—Platonic, Aristotelian, Stoic and Plotinian—may have been the ultimate energizing source of medieval philosophy; but the theology of medieval Christian thinkers acted as a creative and transforming force on the Greek ideas that entered the Latin world. The European philosophy that was transmitted to the sixteenth century, and that was then rethought and reshaped by the classical metaphysicians of the next two centuries, was not Greek but Christian in its basic intuitions and principles; or, to put the matter as Gilson has done, "the point of departure of modern philosophy coincides with the point of arrival of mediaeval theology."[7] Thus, to overlook what happened to Greek philosophy in the Middle Ages, and especially within the several theologies of the thirteenth century, "is to deprive the history of Western thought of its continuity and, by the same token, its intelligibility."[8]

The first thing that should now be obvious is that it is possible to look at medieval philosophy from two distinct but complementary points of view. It should likewise be obvious

6. Ibid., p. 542.
7. Ibid.
8. Ibid.

that the historian who does not balance these points of view properly is in danger of misunderstanding and even distorting the reality that it is nevertheless his purpose to describe in historical terms. When at the end of the ancient section of his monumental *Histoire de la philosophie*, Emile Bréhier wrote that "the development of philosophical thought was not strongly influenced by the coming of Christianity and, to put my point briefly, there is no Christian philosophy,"[9] he was reducing medieval philosophy to the pure survival and penetration of Greek ideas in the medieval Christian world. In other words, for Bréhier, Christianity did not transform man's view of the world or of himself. Up to the sixteenth century, the Greek view lived side by side with Christian spirituality and no new distinctively Christian ideas about the world resulted from the meeting between Greek philosophy and the Christian religion.[10] Christian thinkers thus thought as Greeks, they lived according to the religious and spiritual teaching of their faith, and there was no particular influence of their religion on their philosophy.

It is not an exaggeration to present Bréhier's views in this way. On the contrary, his historical outlook carries its own exaggeration. In denying the historical reality of "Christian

9. E. Bréhier, *Histoire de la philosophie*, vol. 1, pt. 2 (Paris: Presses Universitaires de France, 1948), p. 495.

10. Ibid.

philosophy"—a reality born of the influence of religious notions and sentiments on Greek philosophical ideas—Bréhier was in effect limiting medieval philosophy to the status of an appendix of Greek ideas; and indeed, when in 1937 he published his own *La philosophie du moyen âge*, this is how he described the situation. Philosophy was the creation of Greek reason, and mainly the reason of Aristotle, it survived without change throughout the Middle Ages, and it was influenced only in an external way by revealed truth.[11] And when Bréhier recognized in the very last sentence of his book that, in writing the history of medieval philosophy, he had not entered the domain of theology, he was either distorting the reality he had undertaken to describe as a historian or misunderstanding the kind of ground on which he had been walking.[12]

For (and I here return to Gilson's reflections at the end of his own *History*), as a matter of historical fact there is good reason to think today that medieval philosophy was the creation of theologians. St. Augustine and St. Anselm, William of Auvergne and William of Auxerre, Roger Bacon and Robert Grosseteste, St. Albert the Great and St. Bonaventure, St. Thomas Aquinas, John Duns Scotus and William of Ockham, were all theologians. They philosophized a great deal and even

11. E. Bréhier, *La philosophie du moyen âge* (Paris: A. Michel, 1937), pp. 433–434.
12. Ibid., p. 435.

wrote many purely philosophical discussions. Indeed, they philosophized so much that they created what we commonly call "medieval philosophy"; but they philosophized within their several theologies, they expounded their most distinctive philosophical ideas in their theological writings, and just as distinctively used these ideas for theological purposes. The historian of medieval philosophy cannot very well deny or refuse to accept this fact. The medieval commentaries on Peter Lombard's *Sentences* are theological works. The *Summa Theologiae* of St. Thomas, the so-called *Opus Oxoniense* of John Duns, and the *Ordinatio* of William of Ockham are theological writings and it is in these and similar writings that the main highway of medieval philosophical speculation was built.

Here we are in the presence of an objective historical fact. To many it is also an unpalatable fact. We may condemn the Middle Ages in general, and medieval philosophy in particular, because of this fact; but the one thing that we cannot do about the fact is to deny its reality. For better or for worse, what we call medieval philosophy was created by men who were themselves professional theologians and who, though they knew how to distinguish between philosophy and theology, nevertheless had the interests and the dedication of theologians. Our problem with the modern historians of medieval philosophy really begins at this point. How can a historian of ideas who is himself a rationalist, who therefore dreams of a philosophy that can live by reason alone, not find medieval philosophy an uncongenial historical reality if that reality was created by theologians and is to be found at its best in their theological expositions? On the other hand, how can a historian who is himself a Christian, but who as a Protestant believes that the purity of Christian life and thought should be saved from the total corruption that original sin introduced into the world, not think that medieval thinkers were corrupting Christianity in its very essence by yielding to the intellectual assault of a pagan Aristotle? Finally, how can a historian of ideas who is himself a Christian and a Catholic, but who thinks of philosophy as meticulously distinguished from theology and of theology itself as strictly limited to the world of mystery beyond the power of reason, not find medieval philosophy no less an unmanageable fact?

Of course, it should not seem strange that historians of ideas, having their own philosophical views, should in part write their autobiographies every time they set down the doctrinal story of any man, age, or period of human thought. But if this is not a strange phenomenon, it is one beset by very special and far-reaching dangers for those historians who deal with medieval philosophy. If, like Emile Bréhier, they are rationalists, they have somehow been able to verify their rationalism in and by the history of medieval philosophy as they conceived it. If, like Adolf Harnack of an earlier day, or

Richard Kroner at the present time, they are Protestant theologians interpreting human nature and reason in the light of the Protestant conception of the Fall, then they invite us to think of medieval philosophy as consisting in an impossible and disastrous effort to corrupt and paganize Christian theology.[13] And if they are modern scholastics in their own philosophical views, convinced that the respectability of scholasticism requires the emphatic defense of its autonomy in the presence of theology, then as historians of medieval philosophy they have ignored medieval theology, they have separated the philosophies of medieval thinkers from their theologies and they have presented them to the contemporary world as a self-contained philosophical development in the Middle Ages depending on theology only in a negative and normative way.

It is not my intention to embark upon a general history of modern interpretations of medieval philosophy or to discuss in detail the influence of the personal views of the historians on their interpretation of philosophy in the Middle Ages. But it is important to recognize that we are living at a time when historians are beginning to propose a view of medieval philosophy that succeeds in bringing it into a most unusual focus as a historical reality; and this fact forces upon us serious questions

13. Adolf Harnack, *What is Christianity?*, trans. T. B. Saunders (London: Williams and Norgate, 1903); Richard Kroner, *Speculation and Revelation in the Age of Christian Philosophy* (Philadelphia: The Westminster Press, 1959). Note Chapter X.

as to the very nature of medieval philosophy and theology as well. Evidently, if it is true to say with Gilson that medieval philosophy was created by theologians, and this within the framework of their theologies, so that today it is to be found in their theological writings, then we must begin to think of medieval philosophy as forming a part of medieval theology. Moreover, if it is true that medieval thinkers differed from one another in their theologies, so that they carried out their theological thinking by different rational techniques and with different spiritual objectives in their understanding of their faith, then we must think of scholastic philosophy not only as born within scholastic theology but also as diversified in its structure and teaching according to the personal intellectual character of medieval theologians from St. Anselm to Ockham.

We are now in the presence of the problem of "medieval philosophy" as the student of today sees it both in itself and in the most distinctive overall interpretations it has received in its classical modern historians, namely, Maurice De Wulf, Pierre Mandonnet, and Étienne Gilson.[14] These are the men

---

14. I exclude the work of Canon Van Steenberghen from the present discussion because his position is tied not only to his effort to rehabilitate Siger of Brabant but also to the problem of the interpretation of the famous Munich manuscript (Clm. 9559) discovered by the late Monsignor Grabmann in 1924. Canon Van Steenberghen's historical views on medieval scholasticism, which I have not discussed, can be seen conveniently in his recent publication *The Philosophical Movement in the Thirteenth Century* (Edinburg and New York: Thomas Nelson and Sons, 1955). It will be apparent to the reader that I do not share these views.

who, grounding themselves in the work of many scholars, have given the historical shape to medieval scholasticism that we have grown up with in the last half century. Maurice De Wulf will introduce us to the famous and embattled view, held stubbornly by him for over thirty years, that there was a common scholastic philosophical synthesis in the Middle Ages, distinct and even separate from theology, whose father was St. Anselm in the eleventh century just as the father of anti-scholasticism was John Scotus Erigena in the ninth. Pierre Mandonnet will introduce us to the no less famous view that philosophy in the thirteenth century was divided into three main traditions, namely, the Augustinian, the Albertinian-Thomistic, and the heterodox Averroistic tradition of Siger of Brabant. Father Mandonnet thought that only St. Albert the Great and (even more) St. Thomas Aquinas were able to create a genuine Christian Aristotelianism in the thirteenth century, whereas the Augustinians failed to establish a worthwhile philosophy, while the Averroists held to a philosophy that was as historically Aristotelian in its conclusions as it was heretical in its teachings. Finally, with Étienne Gilson we are invited to think of medieval philosophy as part and parcel of medieval theology and as intensely creative in those precise areas that were of special interest to the theologian, namely, metaphysics and the philosophy of man. With Gilson, moreover, we are likewise invited to think that there were several medieval philosophies not only in the sense that many theologians did not achieve the same results that St. Thomas did, but also in the sense that they followed their own intellectual roads and had no intention of rejoining or even reaching the metaphysical world of St. Thomas himself.

CHAPTER THREE

The Breakdown of the Scholastic Synthesis

III

In 1927 Maurice De Wulf published two articles which, taken together, designate in a most remarkable way his distinctive signature as a historian of medieval philosophy. One of these articles, printed in the first issue of *The New Scholasticism* under the title "Cardinal Mercier: Philosopher," was a eulogy of the Belgian prelate who had died the year before; the other, entitled "Was There a Scholastic Philosophy in the Middle Ages?," was a defense of his famous and cherished thesis that there existed in the Middle Ages a common scholastic synthesis, constituting a coherent body of doctrines, authentically philosophical and distinct from theology, to which St. Thomas Aquinas gave the most perfect expression. In the face of mounting criticism from many quarters, De Wulf, conceding what were in his own eyes minor changes and a question of words, nevertheless reasserted the existence of the same common scholastic synthesis that he had first proposed in 1895 with the publication of his *History of Scholastic Philosophy in the Low Countries*.[1] In reality, what De Wulf defended from 1895 on was the philosophical ideal of a perennial scholastic philosophy that Cardinal Mercier began propounding to the modern world in 1882. It was this scholasticism in whose existence De Wulf the historian believed, whose exposition by Mercier he espoused, and whose history he wrote and defended.

What did De Wulf see in Cardinal Mercier? He saw, apart from the fearless prelate and statesman, a pioneer scholar and philosopher working for a Catholic return to Thomism. Only, let us notice the character of this return. Mercier was returning to Thomism as a free and open philosophy and he "opposed the idea of reducing philosophy to a kind of dogmatic vassalage."[2] Philosophy required independent research and a disinterested pursuit of the whole truth without regard to consequences; it required two characteristics that De Wulf was not slow to see in Mercier, namely, the complete and fearless commitment of philosophy to the world of modern science, its data and its methods, and an equally fearless belief in the harmony of philosophy and theology or religion as distinct disciplines.[3]

1. Maurice De Wulf, "Cardinal Mercier: Philosopher," *The New Scholasticism*, Vol. 1, No. 1 (January 1927), pp. 1–14; "Y eut-il une philosophie scolastique au moyen âge?," *Revue Néo-Scolastique de Philosophie*, Vol. 29 (1927), pp. 5–27.
2. M. De Wulf, "Cardinal Mercier: Philosopher," p. 4.

From this point of view, the return to Thomism was not a backward step, a return to the darkness of the Middle Ages; rather, it was a willingness to let Thomism live and take its chances as a philosophy in the modern world based on the profound conviction "that Thomism was able to maintain a parallel with the other philosophies of our time and to harmonize itself with modern sciences—two new objectives which presided constantly over his [Mercier's] work of reconstruction."[4] Thus did Thomism become Neo-Thomism, and thus did De Wulf discover the perennial scholastic philosophy whose most gifted interpreter St. Thomas Aquinas was. If Mercier was leading men back to St. Thomas Aquinas it was because "the main theories of Thomism—such as pluralism, the horror of monism, respect for personality, the prestige of abstract ideas, the central place of a God elevated above the world and distinct from it—express the deepest aspirations of this [modern] civilization."[5] So understood, "scholasticism is the *philosophia perennis* of the Western world; it will last as long as the civilization which, arising from Greece and transformed by Christianity, has become the spiritual atmosphere which we breathe."[6]

3. Ibid., p. 5.
4. Ibid., pp. 8–9.
5. Ibid., p. 13.
6. Ibid., p. 14.

We are already well within De Wulf's theory of the nature of medieval scholasticism. As he saw it, it was a doctrinal organism that developed slowly across the medieval centuries, beginning in a modest way from the ninth to the twelfth centuries, reaching the fullness of its development in the thirteenth and experiencing a decline in the fourteenth and fifteenth centuries. "For the first time fully conscious of its strength in St. Anselm of Canterbury, it was at full strength later on when St. Thomas Aquinas maintained it in the presence of Arabian doctrines."[7] Scholasticism was thus a philosophical school in the strict sense of the word, but it was not the whole of medieval philosophy since there were heterodox and anti-scholastic currents. As a distinct medieval system, moreover, scholasticism included within itself a number of great principles about God, the world and man. These principles, taken ultimately from Aristotle, had to do with God as pure act, with the structure of creation, involving the notions of potency and act and matter and form, with the doctrine of exemplary divine ideas and the realistic character of human knowledge, and with a conception of man and his conduct whose effect was to pull him within the same dynamic movement toward God that is found in the rest of creation.[8] If the medieval schoolmen

7. M. De Wulf, *Histoire de la philosophie scolastique dans les pays-bas...* (Louvain-Paris, 1895), p. xii.

8. Ibid., pp. xiii–xvii.

differed from one another, it was only after agreeing on the great theses that embodied these doctrines and gave to scholasticism its unity.[9]

These views on medieval scholasticism, strenuously defended by De Wulf in several polemical articles published by him in 1898 and 1899,[10] served as the foundation of the famous *History of Medieval Philosophy* that he brought out in its first edition in the year 1900.[11] The coming of Christianity, he wrote in this book, helped philosophy by fixing the minds of men on the important problems of life. For Christianity "implies a whole system of philosophy whose natural demonstration it makes easier for the intelligence. The essential dependence of man on a creating God, the individuality of creatures, the finality of the universe, the distinction between soul and body, personal immortality—here are a number of great theses that, for many centuries, fill the framework of Catholic philosophy, while at the same time recalling in a special way the most perfect solutions bequeathed by the great minds of antiquity."[12]

9. Ibid., p. xviii.
10. M. De Wulf, "Qu'est-ce que la philosophie scolastique? Les notions fausses et incomplètes," *Revue Néo-Scolastique*, Vol. 5 (1898), pp. 141–153, 282–296; "La synthèse scolastique," *Revue Néo-Scolastique*, Vol. 6 (1899), pp. 41–65, 159–178.
11. M. De Wulf, *Histoire de la philosophie médiévale, précédée d'un aperçu sur la philosophie ancienne*, Cours de Philosophie, publié par D. Mercier, vol. 6 (Louvain-Paris-Brussels, 1900).
12. M. De Wulf, *Histoire de la philosophie médiévale*, p. 130.

We must not exaggerate the influence of Christian dogma on philosophy and think that it removed philosophical liberty. We must rather think of medieval scholasticism, which to De Wulf was "the most important manifestation of medieval thought,"[13] as building on the work of the Fathers and setting out to "construct on the foundation of reason an imposing edifice whose architectonic style was in complete harmony with the principle of Christianity."[14] True enough, scholasticism began by moving on theological soil in the ninth century, but philosophical questions were very soon posed in their own right "without concern for their effect on theology."[15] This means, according to De Wulf, that scholasticism took into account the distinction between philosophy and theology, the diversity of their principles, their methods and their formal objects. At the same time, of course, scholasticism recognized implicitly the relation that held philosophy and theology together.[16]

Let us look again at the scholastic synthesis as De Wulf expounded and defined it when he came to St. Thomas Aquinas. How do we know the constitutive nature of scholasticism? We know it "by the totality of doctrines that it professes on

13. Ibid., p. 131.
14. Ibid. On patristic philosophy, pp. 132–145.
15. Ibid., p. 156.
16. Ibid., p. 179.

the great problems of thought."[17] As thus identified, what is scholasticism? It is, according to De Wulf, a dualistic system of pure act (God) and act-plus-potency (creatures). It involves no monism and no pantheism. It is creationist, its God is a personal one, and its metaphysics of the creature is at once a moderated dynamism (act and potency, form and matter, essence and existence) and an individualism. Its interpretation of the world is finalistic, its psychology is spiritualistic, experimental and objective, and its ethics is eudaemonistic and free. In St. Thomas Aquinas we can see the organic solidarity of the whole scholastic synthesis just as we can see the details in which St. Thomas differed from his contemporaries.[18]

Thus the core of De Wulf s position on the nature of scholastic philosophy, such as he was to maintain it without modification for many years,[19] can be summarized under three chief headings. There was a medieval scholastic philosophy, one and common to all the schoolmen, and Aristotelian in origin and language. Its most perfect expression was to be found in St. Thomas Aquinas. This scholasticism, which

17. Ibid., p. 288; see also p. 147. De Wulf pays particular attention to St. Thomas (pp. 259–290), expounding in connection with his teaching the principles of the scholastic synthesis and noting the doctrines peculiar to him (for his double aim, see p. 262).

18. Ibid., pp. 289–290.

19. See the translation of the widely-used text of the fifth edition (1924). E. Messenger, *History of Mediaeval Philosophy*, vol. 1 (New York: Longmans, Green and Co., 1926), pp. v-viii, 12–21.

is not to be identified with the whole of medieval philosophy, maintained throughout its history a proper distinction between philosophy and theology, so that we can speak of a medieval scholastic philosophy that recognized itself as a separate discipline from medieval theology. It was therefore entirely distinctive of De Wulf to lecture at Harvard University on *Medieval Philosophy Illustrated from the System of Thomas Aquinas*, to mean by his title that "Aquinas is the most striking representative" of the common philosophy of the thirteenth century, and to argue that his aim was to consider scholastic philosophy alone, not theology or dogma. For, though it was true that scholasticism derived its inspiration from theology, yet it was "religious only in the sense in which one can apply the term to art, politics and domestic, social and economic institutions generally." Thus, the philosophy and theology of Thomas Aquinas could be said to complement one another, but "each retains its own independent significance."[20] More specifically and to the point: "it is quite possible to leave aside the religious connections of scholastic philosophy with Catholicism and consider its religious problems only in so far as they enter into a conception of the world and of human life, based upon pure reason."[21]

---

20. M. De Wulf, *Mediaeval Philosophy Illustrated from the System of Thomas Aquinas* (Cambridge: Harvard University Press, 1924), p. 5.
21. Ibid., p. 6.

Such a conviction explains why, in answer to his critics, De Wulf maintained the essentials of his position as late as 1927. When one critic told him in 1926 that "scholasticism is only a word" whereas he himself "thinks of it as a reality," he could only reply that his critic was a nominalist in the use of language.[22] And the issue for De Wulf was certainly not a matter of words; it was a matter of metaphysics. "The doctrinal core of scholasticism," he wrote, "belongs first and foremost to metaphysics, for it is a certain metaphysics that serves as the bone structure for this philosophy."[23] Now, what question in metaphysics was more important than the issue of monism versus pluralism? Medieval scholasticism upheld a pluralistic metaphysics, and it believed in a personal and creating God, a realistic epistemology and a finalistic view of the world of created being, including man. If the thirteenth-century schoolmen differed from one another it was only in the area of secondary issues and after they had accepted this pluralistic metaphysics as a common premise. Here was for De Wulf more than a question of words. He was willing to say: "Since the name 'scholastic synthesis,' which I have used, can bring to mind the idea of a finished structure, perhaps it is preferable to

22. M. DeWulf, "Y eut-il une philosophie scolastique au moyen âge?," p. 20. See G. Théry, O.P., in *Revue des sciences philosophiques et théologiques*, Vol. 15 (1926), p. 549.

23. M. De Wulf, "Y eut-il une philosophie scolastique au moyen âge?," pp. 12–13.

substitute for it those of a 'common' or 'collective patrimony' of the scholastics." But in thus giving up the word "synthesis" De Wulf did not give up what he had meant by it. Admitting that not all the medieval schoolmen shared in the same way in their common patrimony, he argued that their differences proved that the schoolmen "of the thirteenth century are *philosophers more or less* according as they enter *more or less* the interpretation of these rational doctrines" to be found in the common patrimony. For example, St. Bonaventure is less a philosopher than St. Thomas because he freed himself less than did St. Thomas from religious preoccupations; for "a man is a philosopher to the extent to which he seeks a *rational* explanation of the enigmas of the real."[24]

What could be clearer? If it needed proving, this conclusion shows that De Wulf was faithful to the ideal of scholastic philosophy that he saw in Cardinal Mercier, and he was faithful to it even at the moment when he was making his *apologia* as a historian before his colleagues. Scholasticism was for him a synthesis because in its perfect and proper form it was the philosophy of St. Thomas Aquinas; what is more, as a philosophy Thomism maintained the full and pure rationality of its doctrine. From this point of view, St. Bonaventure shared in the same metaphysical synthesis as did St. Thomas, but less

24. Ibid., pp. 21–22 (author's italics).

perfectly so, and this is precisely why he was less perfectly a philosopher, that is, less perfectly free from religious occupations and therefore less perfectly involved in pure philosophy.

In his monumental work entitled *Siger of Brabant and Latin Averroism in the Thirteenth Century*, which he first published in 1899 and issued in an expanded two-volume second edition in 1908 and 1911,[25] the Dominican scholar Pierre Mandonnet did not entirely depart from the view of Maurice De Wulf even though he rejected the idea of a common medieval scholastic synthesis. As he saw it, the so-called scholastic synthesis of De Wulf was in reality the Christian Aristotelian tradition established by St. Albert the Great and St. Thomas Aquinas and by them alone. The Augustinian tradition rejected Aristotle, while the heterodox Latin Averroists accepted his philosophy as interpreted by Averroes even at the price of having a philosophy in conflict with their Christian faith. If we leave aside Latin Averroism,[26] the issue between De Wulf and Father Mandonnet consists in determining why the latter did not think that Augustinianism was either a philosophy properly so-called or a philosophy that belonged to the Christian Aristotelian tradition.

25. Pierre Mandonnet, O. P., *Siger de Brabant et l'averroïsme latin au XIIIe siècle*, 2nd ed., 2 vols. (Louvain: Institut Supérieur de Philosophie, 1911 [study], 1908 [texts]).

26. Ibid., vol. 1, ch. 4–7.

According to Father Mandonnet, the reigning doctrinal tradition in the theological world of the early thirteenth century was Platonic-Augustinian. The theologians who were disciples of this tradition wished to keep Aristotle out of theology. Following the spirit of the time, the early Dominicans were themselves hostile to the introduction of philosophy and Aristotle into theology. Nevertheless, though resisted, the study of Aristotle entered the Dominican order through the work of St. Albert the Great and his pupil St. Thomas Aquinas. In fact, Albert won for Aristotle the first battle of the thirteenth century: with Albert, Aristotle entered the Christian theological world. St. Thomas was to win the second battle, namely, the battle of determining what the text of Aristotle meant. In the second half of the thirteenth century, which saw the rise of Latin Averroism, St. Thomas undertook a minute exegesis of the text of Aristotle translated from the original Greek in order to prove against the Averroists the error of an anti-Christian interpretation of Aristotle and the correctness of a Christian Aristotelianism.[27]

The consequences of the Aristotelian revolution of St. Thomas Aquinas were to be enormous within the realm of Christian theology. At this point we meet Father Mandonnet's description of the Augustinian school that both resisted the

27. Ibid., pp. 28–29, 37–39, 39–42.

entry of Aristotle into theology and did not itself have a proper notion of philosophy. The Augustinians were a diffuse body of thinkers, held together by a number of more or less characteristic theses taken from St. Augustine and ultimately from Plato. Augustinianism as a whole was marked by "an absence of a formal distinction between the domain of philosophy and that of theology, that is, between the order of rational truths and that of revealed truth. At times, the two orders are fused to make up a total wisdom, on the basis of the principle that the truths possessed by the ancient philosophers are the result of a divine illumination and on this ground are part of revelation as a whole. At other times, the domains of philosophy and theology are acknowledged as juridically distinct, but in fact no principle is ever formulated that can safeguard this distinction. There is, moreover, a similar tendency to blur the formal separation of nature and grace. It is this fact of the absorption of the object of philosophy in that of theology that has furnished the pretext and also the semi-justification for the often-repeated charge that the scholastics have not known how to take up the examination of scientific problems independently of dogma, and even that their philosophy should not find a place in the history of this science. But this accusation, which has a real foundation in the case of Augustinian theologians, is groundless in the case of the Thomistic school, for which the object of science and the object of faith are defined strictly and declared to be irreducible to one another, and the treatises of pure science are executed without ever touching on a theological question."[28]

Thus, whereas for De Wulf the metaphysical synthesis effected by St. Thomas Aquinas was the perfect form of a commonly held scholastic philosophy, with Father Mandonnet it became the unique possession of the Thomistic school, including with reservations St. Albert himself. Judging by the preceding paragraph, we must say that Father Mandonnet agreed with De Wulf on the ideal of a pure scholastic philosophy created by the unaided reason and fully distinct from theology by virtue of its object. The Augustinian school—the seculars, the early Dominicans, and the Franciscans[29]—not only did not distinguish properly between theology and philosophy but, by accepting the Platonic metaphysics of St. Augustine, tended to efface that distinction. In this they were not following the scientific revolution created by St. Albert and

28. Ibid., pp. 55–57. See M. De Wulf, *Le Traité "De Unitate Formae" de Gilles de Lessines* (Louvain: Institut Supérieur, 1901), pp. 10ff., especially p. 21, note 3.

29. P. Mandonnet, *Siger de Brabant*, vol. 1, pp. 51–55. Among the specifically Platonic theses of the Augustinian school Father Mandonnet listed the priority of the good over the true and the will over the intellect; the notion of God as the highest good rather than as the first and necessary being; the need for a special divine illumination for true knowledge; the hylomorphic composition of spiritual substances; the notion that matter is, not pure potentiality, but a minimum but positive actuality; the notion that the human soul does not have a true union with the body since it is only a new form in an already existing and living composite; and the doctrine of a plurality of substantial forms in man (ibid., pp. 56–57).

St. Thomas out of Aristotle. Indeed, the Platonic tendencies of the Augustinian school mixed religion and philosophy and produced a Neoplatonic syncretism that had nothing to do with Aristotle and that in fact was not even a proper part of the history of philosophy.[30]

If, with this conclusion, we can say that Father Mandonnet denied the existence of a common metaphysical backbone in medieval scholasticism, let us also remember wherein he agreed with the eminent Belgian historian. With De Wulf he believed in a pure Thomistic philosophy, even though he did not think that the Augustinians knew how to hold a "pure" philosophy. Their philosophy was Platonic and not Aristotelian in its foundations; it therefore tended to deny the possibility of the distinction of the sciences as proposed in the Aristotelian tradition and as used by St. Thomas to establish philosophy and theology as diversely inspired disciplines.

At this point begins the evolution of medieval philosophy such as we have known it since the 1920's, the period influenced and then dominated by the historical views of Étienne Gilson. I am not concerned to describe it here if only because, as part of our intellectual world, it is relatively better known to us. In noting a few among the larger developments of the last four decades I wish simply to underline the fact that we are

30. Ibid., p. 55, n. 2.

today nearer to understanding the dilemma that has plagued modern scholasticism; and we are nearer because we are able to appreciate its medieval origins in a fuller and better way than were the scholastics of eighty years ago. Our "nearness" has been produced by the steady advance of historians from De Wulf to Gilson and by the progressive elimination from the history of medieval philosophy of the notion of a common scholastic synthesis, then of the notion of a self-contained Christian Aristotelianism attributed to St. Albert the Great and St. Thomas Aquinas, and finally of the notion of a distinctly articulated Thomistic philosophy living in one wing of St. Thomas' mind while his theology lives in another.

In 1924 Gilson wrote his now classic book on St. Bonaventure, in which he established among other things that the Seraphic Doctor had no intention of being either an imitation St. Thomas or a follower of St. Thomas in any sense. He wished to be an Augustinian in theology and in philosophy, and his most distinctive doctrinal theses tended to separate him from St. Thomas just as they revealed the existence of a coherent philosophy serving the purposes of a devout theology.[31] At the same time, other historical studies were beginning to show that the Christian Aristotelian synthesis attributed to St. Albert and St. Thomas was not a common synthesis at all. St. Albert respected but did not adopt the philosophy of his illustrious pupil, and his metaphysical views were no simple amalgam of Platonic and Aristotelian notions to be purified by that same pupil, but a Neoplatonic structure of remarkable sophistication and coherence. St. Thomas, in turn, departed from his master not only on specific points of doctrine but also in his basic metaphysics of being and existence.[32]

While these developments were going on, medievalists were showing still another source of division in the supposed community of medieval scholastic philosophy. In 1938 a Belgian scholar published a magnificent book on Henry of Ghent in which he set forth the general outlines of a metaphysical doctrine that was neither Augustinian nor Aristotelian in the recognized sense in which these terms were being applied to St. Bonaventure and St. Thomas.[33] It seemed to be a new combination of Augustinian and Aristotelian elements, inspired by the philosopher Avicenna, and destined to be

31. É. Gilson, *La philosophie de Saint Bonaventure* (Paris: Librairie Philosophique J. Vrin, 1924). See the critical review of P. Mandonnet, in *Bulletin Thomiste*, Vol. 3, No. 2 (March 1926), pp. 50–54, especially p. 52.

32. See Bernard J. Muller-Thym, *The Establishment of the University of Being in the Doctrine of Meister Eckhart of Hochheim* (New York: Sheed and Ward, 1939), pp. 28–67; also, A. C. Pegis, *St. Thomas and the Problem of the Soul in the Thirteenth Century* (Toronto: St. Michael's College, 1934), pp. 77–120; É. Gilson, "L'Ame raisonnable chez Albert le Grand," *Archives d'histoire doctrinale et littéraire du moyen âge*, Vol. 14 [1943–1945], pp. 5–72; *History of Christian Philosophy in the Middle Ages*, pp. 277–294, 666–673; B. de Solages, "La coherence de la métaphysique de l'âme d'Albert le Grand," *Melanges offerts au R. P. Fernand Cavallera* (Toulouse: Bibliothèque de l'Institut Catholique, 1948), pp. 367–400.

33. J. Paulus, *Henri de Gand. Essai sur les tendances de sa métaphysique* (Paris: Librairie Philosophique J. Vrin, 1938).

known among historians by the rather barbarous name of "Avicennizing Augustinism." The great Duns Scotus was one of the disciples of this new metaphysical doctrine.[34] In the Subtle Doctor there lived an Augustinianism that was free of certain theses held as Augustinian by St. Bonaventure—for example, the notion of seminal principles and the embattled doctrine of the necessity of a special divine illumination for the existence of true knowledge in man. It was Aristotle as interpreted by Avicenna who had given to the Subtle Doctor this freedom from the older Augustinianism of the school of St. Bonaventure; but it was the same Aristotle as interpreted by the same Avicenna who separated Duns from the Aristotelianism of St. Thomas Aquinas on many crucial questions and especially the question of the starting point of a metaphysics that would lead to the Christian God.

These and other important doctrinal differences among the medieval schoolmen are commonly recognized by historians today. Not all historians acknowledge or emphasize the same differences, nor do they all evaluate or explain the differences in the same way. There is no doubt however that the common scholastic synthesis as well as the common

34. On Avicenna and Duns Scotus there is the classic paper of É. Gilson, "Avicenne et le point de départ de Duns Scot," *Archives d'histoire doctrinale et littéraire du moyen âge*, Vol. 2 (1927), pp. 89–149. On Gilson's general conclusions on the interpretation of Duns Scotus, see his *Jean Duns Scot. Introduction à ses positions fondamentales* (Paris: Librairie Philosophique J. Vrin, 1952), pp. 625–669.

Aristotelian inspiration of this synthesis have disappeared as serious interpretations of medieval thinkers. St. Bonaventure, St. Albert the Great, St. Thomas Aquinas and Duns Scotus—to take the four greatest of the medieval schoolmen—built four distinct metaphysical syntheses in their respective theologies, all recognizable in their differences and all coherent within themselves. If they all spoke the basic philosophical language of Aristotle, they managed to express four different metaphysical doctrines with it, as diverse in their primary intuitions as they were distinctively dependent on various combinations of St. Augustine, Aristotle and Avicenna. Medieval philosophy, as we see it today, is a community of philosophizing theologians rather than a common synthesis. Moreover, as several diverse and diversely inspired doctrinal movements, it has required of its historians the invention of new terms to characterize and designate the metaphysical differences among the doctrines of thirteenth- and fourteenth-century schoolmen.

CHAPTER FOUR

Philosophy in the World of Theology

IV

But perhaps the most significant change in our historical perspective concerns, not the emergence of several medieval doctrinal syntheses, but the status of philosophy itself in the medieval world and especially within the work of each of the great theologians. In 1932 Étienne Gilson published the text of his Gifford Lectures under the title *The Spirit of Mediaeval Philosophy*.[1] These lectures aimed to show not only how much medieval theologians transformed Greek philosophical ideas, and what different doctrinal roads they followed in this transformation, but also and especially how much the work of transforming Greek philosophy owed to the inspiration and the impulse of the Christian revelation. If the historians of medieval philosophy, therefore, had step by step proved to us that a common scholastic synthesis never existed in the Middle Ages, Étienne Gilson, who played a leading part in that story, has played an even more unique role in the establishment of another notion, namely, that of "Christian philosophy."

Though it be true that medieval theologians did not create or share in a common philosophical synthesis, it is also true that they felt the influence of a common religious teaching and inspiration. The teaching of the Christian revelation impelled their minds, amid otherwise great differences, to think their way toward a God Whose name was he who is; to express in a rational way the fact that this God was a creator and a providence, free and omnipotent in His immediate government over the universe; to find an adequate formula for the notion of man as a unitary substance composed of an intellectual soul and an organic body; and to give an account of the long and laborious effort of mankind to establish a human society on earth as part of its journey to the heavenly Jerusalem. This religious teaching among medieval theologians was not a

---

1. É. Gilson, *L'Esprit de la philosophie médiévale*, 2 vols. (Paris: Librairie Philosophique J. Vrin, 1932); English trans. A. H. C. Downes, *The Spirit of Mediaeval Philosophy* (New York: Charles Scribner's Sons, 1934). The companion to this book is, naturally, *Christianisme et philosophie* (Paris: Librairie Philosophique J. Vrin, 1936); English trans. R. McDonald, C.S.B., *Christianity and Philosophy* (New York and London: Sheed and Ward, 1939).

   I have tried elsewhere to present the main outlines of Gilson's thought as a historian, a philosopher, and a Thomist: "Gilson and Thomism," *Thought*, Vol. 21, No. 82 (September 1946), pp. 435–454; *A Gilson Reader* (Garden City, NY: Hanover House and Image Books, 1957), pp. 7–20. On Gilson as a philosopher and historian see also the symposium *Étienne Gilson, philosophe de la chrétienté. Rencontres*, No. 30 (Paris: Les Editions du Cerf, 1949), pp. 25–102.

common body of doctrines but a common spiritual ferment; it was faith working within the human mind, urging it both to believe and to express, in the national language of Aristotle, the intellectual shape and character of the Christian world in all its creaturehood, from its origin to its destiny in God. No, there was not a common philosophy in the Middle Ages, but there was a common religious and theological effort to teach Christian doctrine through the instrumentality of philosophical notions taken from Aristotle. That is why, though Gilson has been more responsible than any other historian for undoing the thesis of a common scholastic philosophical synthesis, he has also been distinctively responsible for recognizing the reality of what he has called "Christian philosophy." I suggest that Christian philosophy, as explained by Gilson, is the historical successor to the earlier and untenable thesis of a common scholasticism. It is, when considered historically, a much more impressive thesis and a more elusive one. That is why the thesis itself, which has been much discussed and much misunderstood, is worth our most serious attention as students of medieval thought.[2]

---

2. Among Professor Gilson's recent writings bearing on the problem of Christian philosophy and the role of Thomism, the following are significant as revealing their author's present point of view:

(1) A. C. Pegis, ed., "What is Christian Philosophy?," in *A Gilson Reader* (Garden City, NY: Hanover House, 1957), pp. 177–191.

Here I wish only to point out that the most paradoxical aspects of "Christian philosophy" are only now beginning to appear. For it remains true that the schoolmen did not learn philosophy from Aristotle in order to become philosophers, even Christian philosophers; they learned philosophy in order to use it as the appropriate rational tool in the formation of what was for them a Christian theology. Those who have objected to the view that the philosophies of medieval thinkers were *Christian* philosophies must now contend with the even more difficult view that these philosophies were created by theologians within theology and for the purposes of theology; in short, they were created as parts of theology itself. If this is true, then we must ask ourselves exactly what it was that took place in the thirteenth century when the Latinized writings

---

(2) *Elements of Christian Philosophy* (Garden City, NY: Doubleday & Company, Inc., 1960), pp. 11–42.

(3) *Introduction à la philosophie chrétienne* (Paris: Librairie Philosophique J. Vrin, 1960).

(4) "St. Thomas and the Peace of Theology," in *Paths to Peace*, Four lectures presented at Rockhurst College for 1960–1961 (Kansas City, MO, 1961), pp. 12–25.

(5) *Le philosophe et la théologie* (Paris: Librairie Arthème Fayard, 1960); English trans. C. Gilson, *The Philosopher and Theology* (New York: Random House, 1962).

(6) "De la connaissance du principe," *Revue de métaphysique et de morale*, No. 4 (1961), pp. 373–397.

Two critical discussions of Gilson and the problem of Christian philosophy may be mentioned: M. Nédoncelle, *Existe-t-il une philosophie chéetienne?* (Paris: Libraire A Fayard, 1956), English trans. I. Trethowan, *Is There a Christian Philosophy?* (New York: Hawthorne Books, 1961); E. A. Sillem, "Perspectives on Christian Philosophy," *The Clergy Review*, Vol. 46, No. 3 (March 1961), pp. 149–165; reprinted in *Philosophy Today*, Vol. 5, No. 1 (March 1961), pp. 3–13.

of Aristotle were circulating in the newly-established University of Paris. We used to say that what then took place was that Greek philosophy was received into the Christian world, subjected to a period of examination and correction, and then assimilated within Christian thought and culture.[3] From such a point of view, the main work of the thirteenth century consisted in Christianizing Greek philosophy and especially the philosophy of Aristotle.

But what if the perspective involved in this interpretation is not correct? Let us suppose, for example, that, though the reception of Aristotle was an undeniably crucial problem in the thirteenth century, it was not the most important or the most critical situation created by the arrival of his Latinized texts. Suppose, to carry the point a bit further, that in the presence of Aristotelianism the primary intellectual task of St. Thomas Aquinas as a thirteenth-century theologian was the construction of a theology suited to the work of meeting the challenge posed by Aristotelianism, so that the assimilation of the Greek Aristotle and his intellectual world was no more than the external moment of a much deeper internal change within Christian thought itself. From such a point of view,

3. For a summary of the action of the Church on Aristotle in the thirteenth century, see É. Gilson, *History of Christian Philosophy in the Middle Ages*, pp. 244–246, 654–655. For an effort to explain the constructive purpose and spirit of the Church's prohibitions, see M. Grabmann, *I Papi del Duecento e l'Aristotelismo*, 2 vols. (Rome: Gregorian University Press, 1941, 1946).

the chief task of the thirteenth century was nothing less than the creation of a Christian intellectualism, that is to say, the creation of an intellectual expression of Christian teaching that was religious in its roots and intellectual in its form and structure. For how could it be Christian without being rooted in revelation? And how could it be intellectual without using the very same language of reason that had entered the Christian world in the writings of Aristotle? How, indeed, could Christianity have an authentic encounter with Aristotelian philosophy unless the encounter involved a true intellectual confrontation between the world of belief and the world of philosophy? This was possible only on one condition, namely, if between revelation and philosophy, between the Christian message and the message of Aristotle, a new and daring intellectual edifice was built by Christians themselves—the message of revelation in the form of a philosophy, expressing itself in the Aristotelian language of *being*. And this is what the thirteenth century accomplished. Between revelation and philosophy it created a new Christian reality, a metaphysically-ordered theology, a theology that installed the thinking of Aristotle within faith and built a bridge from revelation to reason.

I would like to suggest that the main accomplishment of the thirteenth century was the establishment of what may be called the "Christianity of the universities" as distinguished from the "Christianity of the monasteries." The transition from the Christianity of the monasteries to the Christianity of the universities, or, to say it differently, from the religious world of the Cistercian and Victorine monks to the intellectual university world of St. Bonaventure, St. Albert and St. Thomas, involved a revolutionary internal transformation of Christian thought itself. If, with the twelfth-century sons of St. Benedict, the Christian world had been a cloister of devout contemplation, seeking not knowledge but spiritual love, not growth in rationality but an increase in devotion, not the synoptic vision of all being but the more elevated praise and enjoyment of God, in the thirteenth century Christianity became a doctrine to teach in the language and with the method of Aristotle. The twelfth-century monks had been humble pilgrims building spiritual arks or waiting for the birth of a spiritual Benjamin, the gift of divine contemplation. By contrast, St. Bonaventure (at least for a time) and St. Thomas Aquinas were university professors, giving to Christian truths a human and rational expression and therefore formulating a theology that spoke for the Christian revelation in a way that was fully grounded in metaphysics and the procedures of human rationality.

The thirteenth century was the age in which man came alive within Christianity in the constitution and the voice of his intellectual nature. He learned to speak with the science of his intellect within the mystery of his religious faith. The result was the establishment of a new intellectual Christianity, as well as a new Christian intelligence, anchored in revelation for its truth and in philosophical understanding for its expression and its techniques. The men who created such a Christianity were theologians, their work was theology, and the books in which they gave expression to this Christianity and this theology were a new form of Christian literature, namely, the theological *Summae*. These theologians were the true scholastics and their work was scholasticism, that is to say, Christian teaching speaking the language of metaphysics. As theologians, the scholastics were distinguished by the use of philosophy (mainly, though not exclusively, Aristotelian philosophy) as their chief intellectual tool, by the observance of philosophical canons in their mode of exposition and explanation, and by the effort to elevate philosophical procedure in an appropriate way to the service of revealed truth.

There are important consequences for our interpretation of both medieval philosophy and modern scholasticism if these conclusions should happen to be true. They seem true enough to propose as a working hypothesis at the present time. "Medieval philosophy" was created by thirteenth-century theologians as the intellectual structure and tool they developed for the exposition of Christian religious truths when they came face to face with an Aristotelian and even pagan philosophical view of the world. The philosophy created by medieval theologians was, moreover, the technical medium with which they aimed to express the monastic Christianity of the Fathers in a truly intellectual way and to formulate the truths of the Christian religion, so far as this was possible, as a humanly communicable and teachable doctrine. As a theological tool, philosophy lived and functioned within the several theologies of the professors in the faculty of theology at Paris and elsewhere; and it was naturally shaped by, and in turn shaped, these theologies in their very divergences from one another. Such as it was, the philosophy of each medieval theologian was part of his theology; however recognizable in its rationality, it was not separated from the theological body in which it was developed as a theological instrument. Nor should we be surprised that, as an instrument of theology, philosophy was influenced by its religious state and service. It became a "Christian philosophy" in the sense that its religious employment opened it toward the world of revealed truth and enabled it to be at home in such a world. Its religious employment also gave it a direction, including perceptions and intuitions, that it would otherwise not have had, just as this same Christian service tended to expand philosophical speculation within those areas that were of professional interest to the theologian. For the same reason, we should not be surprised that in the hands of the theologian philosophy likewise tended to reflect not only the Christian character of his work or the concentration of his efforts in specific centers of interest, but also his willingness to stop short in the examination of certain questions and to measure his philosophical involvement or curiosity by the needs of his immediate theological purpose.

And this is the point we seem to have reached in our day. The fact that we have come so far in our interpretation of what is called medieval philosophy may suggest some cautious optimism for the immediate future; but it should also give us some rather astonishing intellectual food for thought. The idea that medieval philosophy was the creation of theologians is only less astonishing than the further idea that this philosophy was created as part of theology for theological purposes. Here we are in the presence of a truly extraordinary phenomenon and one that will require a considerable reconstruction in perspective if we are to see it as it really was. To repeat, it *is* extraordinary that what we call medieval philosophy was created as theology—as mystery speaking the language of metaphysics, and therefore as metaphysics assumed in the service of mystery. The more we see medieval philosophy in this way the more we are driven to recognize the speculative power of medieval theologians and the true signature of the thirteenth century. This was not primarily the century in which Christian thinkers learned from Aristotle how to be philosophers. This was, first and foremost, the century in which, face to face with the purely philosophical wisdom of Aristotle, and with all the doctrinal and technical challenges embodied in that wisdom,

Christian thinkers created a theological wisdom in answer to it, a wisdom rooted in revelation but in communication with the metaphysical world of Aristotelianism through its own human intellectual structure. We are the heirs of this theological wisdom of the thirteenth century and we have lived, as did others before us, in the intellectual world and on the doctrinal capital created by it.

CHAPTER FIVE

Ambivalence of Scholasticism

V

IF MEDIEVAL PHILOSOPHY as the creation of theologians is becoming an increasingly complex exegetical problem for its modern historians, it is likewise posing no less challenging issues for the modern scholastic philosopher. I refer to these issues because the present-day scholastic, having lost direct contact with his medieval origins, no longer remembers or appreciates that he is the intellectual child of medieval theologians; indeed, since the days of Descartes, he has rather wished to live in the modern world as a modern philosopher, in a state of freedom and emancipation from the theology that produced him. But the last eighty years have helped us to regain some contact with the Middle Ages. If around 1880 it seemed reasonable to think of scholasticism as a pure philosophy, and this in the name of its rationality, today historical facts suggest that we ought to think of it as a religious philosophy in the sense that its rationality was born and fostered in a religious climate. There never was a "pure" scholastic philosophy in the Middle Ages, and the same theologians who knew how to distinguish between philosophy and theology in the name of their respective formal objects, nevertheless established that distinction, not to develop philosophies outside their theologies, or to become themselves philosophers, but to respect the nature of philosophy at the moment of using it to create their theologies. The problem that medieval philosophy poses, therefore, is not satisfied by distinguishing between philosophy and theology, since that distinction is not at stake. The problem is what may be called the ambivalence of medieval philosophy precisely as philosophy.

As a philosophy born in a religious climate, under the inspiration of a Christian view of the world and of man, scholasticism was bound to be a Christian philosophy, a philosophy in which we can recognize both the Christian leaven and the natural expression of human intelligence. But medieval philosophy was more than a Christian reality, it was also an instrument of theology; and while its theological employment was indeed a Christian service, it was also a doctrinal engagement beyond the range of philosophy as such. And this is the ambivalence in medieval philosophy that we must consider in our own day, namely, the difference between its Christian character as a philosophy and its theological state of service. By not taking into account his own history, the modern scholastic has transformed the ambivalence of medieval philosophy into a cruel dilemma. Medieval theologians created philosophy, or sometimes simply borrowed it from Aristotle, in order to express religious truths in a religious way, in short, to formulate a theology. There is philosophy in their work, and even a Christian philosophy; for, to mention one example, how could they have undertaken to speak of a God Who said that His name was Being unless they made the metaphysics of Aristotle lead to such a God, whatever Aristotle himself may have thought? Only, this Christian philosophy was the voice of the theologian articulating religious truths, including the highest mysteries of Christianity; it was a religious tool and, by so much, not a philosophy but a theology. The ambivalence of medieval philosophy lies here. By as much as it was a theology, there is a sense in which it was not a philosophy: it did not, in fact, have the autonomous state of expression proper to a philosophy. It had, instead, the auxiliary state of a theological instrument, existing for the purposes of the theologian, serving his aims and thereby following the direction that his work and interests imposed on it. Have we measured the meaning of such a situation? Have we considered the nature and character of a philosophy living under these conditions? Let us, once more, look at the facts in the case.

Created as part of a theological effort, at once religious and rational, to formulate an intellectual Christianity in the presence of Greek philosophy—by which I mean a religious intellectualism in the presence of a pagan philosophical intellectualism—the philosophy of medieval theologians had two distinguishing characteristics that ought to be clearly noted and just as clearly set off from one another.

In the first place, it was a "Christian philosophy," fully deserving both the noun and the adjective in its name. It fully deserved the name *philosophy* because it was a genuine work of human intelligence functioning according to its own natural light. It also deserved to be called *Christian* because, at the very same time, this philosophical edifice was built under the influence and the inspiration of revealed truth. In short, we can see a Christian intelligence at work in St. Thomas Aquinas, at once fully an intelligence in its life and fully Christian in the expression and growth of that life.

But, in the second place, the philosophy of medieval theologians was not only as philosophy Christian in its inspiration, it also existed within theology in order to serve the exposition of faith. Considered as functioning within such a service, this philosophy became, by reason of its employment, a part of theology—I mean to say a functioning instrument of theological exposition. In short, medieval philosophy was both a Christian philosophy and an instrument of Christian theology. This is the ambivalence in medieval philosophy to which I have referred and which we must try to understand.

Thus, to take up a crucial instance, if it be the case that St. Thomas Aquinas, as a thirteenth-century theologian, did not set out to become a Christian philosopher or to Christianize Aristotle in the process of assimilating his philosophy; if, instead, Aristotelianism posed for him an intellectual crisis to which the proper answer was the creation of a Christian theology, a religious intellectualism, then perhaps we are in a position to recognize both the nature of our indebtedness to the Angelic Doctor and the precise conditions under which, because he was something greater than a philosopher, he can be for us today a teacher in philosophy.

Let us begin with the premise that St. Thomas was by profession a theologian, not a philosopher. Let us add the premise that this theologian created a philosophy within his theology in order to aid, and indeed to make possible, the human expression of revealed truth. In the third place, let us admit that a philosophy so created was Christian in its spirit, its use and its interests, even though as Christian it remained philosophy in its substance since it observed the principles of philosophical thinking. That is why indeed we call it a Christian philosophy. But, in the fourth place, let us also and especially recognize that this Christian philosophy was engaged in a theological task dictated for it by the specific service it was asked to perform and not at all by its own nature as philosophy even when we add the adjective "Christian." Thus, we are forced to distinguish within the philosophy of a medieval theologian the fact that it was Christian from the further fact that it was a theological instrument.

To bring the point down to a concrete case, let us recognize that in the *Summa Theologiae* of St. Thomas Aquinas there is at work a Christian philosophy in the service of faith. This philosophy is Christian, it is Christian as philosophy, but, more than this, it is a servant of theology. This is an extraordinary fact that the student of St. Thomas cannot but emphasize and that the modern Thomist does not have the right to ignore or to neglect. Located within his theology for the sake of that theology, the philosophy of St. Thomas gives abundant evidence of both its Christian spirit and its theological occupation. How often, for example, did St. Thomas not find it suitable to his purpose merely to report in a compressed or limited form the arguments of the philosophers? Not to insist on the five ways, which are reports of five arguments for the existence of God drawn from diverse metaphysical doctrines, what are we to do with St. Thomas' own commentary on what is commonly called the treatise on man? St. Thomas himself points out that this series of questions in the *Pars Prima* has a theological emphasis and is, for the same reason, philosophically incomplete. Now, if any thinker ever believed in the essential integrity of man, in the oneness of soul and body and their life, that thinker was surely St. Thomas. It makes no difference in the present discussion whether he held such a doctrine for Aristotelian reasons or for reasons of his own creation. To St. Thomas, soul and body were parts, and man was the whole of which they were parts; it was this whole, taken in its integrity, that should have been the object of study. And yet the very same St. Thomas who defended the unity of man tells us that the *consideratio theologi* deals with the nature of man from the side of the soul, not that of the body, except according to the relation that the body has to the soul. On at least two other occasions within the same discussion St. Thomas pointed out the way in which the *consideratio theologi* shaped and directed his interest in the study of man.[1] If these restrictions mean anything they mean that St. Thomas knowingly limited his study of man to

1. The three texts on the *consideratio theologi* are evidently intended as organizational rubrics by St. Thomas himself. The first concerns the theologian's approach to the study of human nature. "Naturam autem hominis considerare pertinet ad Theologum ex parte animae, non autem ex parte corporis, nisi secundum habitudinem quam habet corpus ad animam. Et ideo prima consideratio circa animam versabitur" (*ST* I, q. 75, prol.). A similar restriction applies to the study of the powers of the soul; it is only by an extension of his interest that the theologian studies all the powers: "Ad considerationem autem theologi pertinet inquirere specialiter solum de potentiis intellectivis et appetitivis in quibus virtutes inveniuntur. Sed quia cognitio harum potentiarum quodammodo dependet ex aliis, ideo nostra consideratio de potentiis animae in speciali erit tripartita" (*ST* I, q. 78, prol.). The acts and habits of the soul are approached in the same way. "Consequenter considerandum est de actibus et habitibus animae, quantum ad potentias intellectivas et appetitivas; aliae enim potentiae non pertinent directe ad considerationem theologi" (*ST* I, q. 84, prol.).

the soul and for theological reasons centered it in the study of the soul. And, in point of fact, there is no direct study of the human body in the treatise on man such as one would expect in a complete and balanced examination of the nature of man, nor is there explicitly formulated a unified approach to man as man. Why not? Evidently because, as a theologian, St. Thomas did not think it necessary to engage in one.

The point at issue should be clear. The philosophy that we find in the *Summa* and call "Thomistic" must be described as not only *Christian* but also *theological:* it has the mode of employment, development and exposition that suits St. Thomas' theological purpose. Let us, therefore, consider carefully, in this crucial instance, the difference between the Christian state of philosophy and its theological employment or service. No doubt, it is one and the same Christian philosophy that St. Thomas Aquinas uses for the purpose of theology; but it remains that the reasons that make it Christian are not identical with the reasons that make it theological.

The historian of medieval philosophy in general, and of St. Thomas in particular, must emphasize this point because modern scholasticism has lived in almost complete unawareness of it. Those who built philosophical manuals by collecting texts from the theological writings of St. Thomas did not see that a philosophy that owed its existence to the theological service for which it was intended was a philosophy formed by that service and therefore reflecting within itself the conditions of its original employment. We must not confuse what is Christian in the philosophy to be found in the *Summa* with what is *in addition* theological in the use that St. Thomas made of it. Because St. Thomas was a theologian, philosophy as he employed it was bound to show, at one and the same time, both the imprint of its theological service and the internal marks of its own nature. Its theological service is indeed part of the concrete expression of the philosophy in the *Summa,* but the reason for this fact is that St. Thomas was a theologian, the reason is not that he grounded the service in the nature of philosophy as such, even when we call it Christian. The *Summa* is full of summarized arguments, of philosophical questions seen obliquely and in midstream, of reported philosophical discussions, and of philosophy itself seen from the heights of theology. There is philosophy in these reports and summaries, and we can see it, but the arguments have a state of presentation that is in view of St. Thomas' immediate theological purpose.

There are therefore good reasons for distinguishing clearly between philosophy as shaped theologically by St. Thomas himself and philosophy as the Christian reality we find in his writings within the theological mission of their author. To repeat, we cannot divorce St. Thomas' philosophy either from its Christian climate or from its theological service: it will remain forever a Christian philosophy ministering to a theology. However, we can and should distinguish the philosophy in the *Summa* as the work of human intelligence from its theological state of realization; just as when we see St. Thomas carrying the ideas of Plato and Aristotle, or Avicenna and Averroes, beyond their limits but in continuity with their intuitions and in contact with his own religious beliefs, we can recognize that philosophy itself is being shaped by its Christian climate under our very eyes. Moreover, not only can we not divorce St. Thomas' philosophy from the historical conditions of its existence—from his intellectual vision, his Christian faith, his theological dedication—but our only chance of remaining faithful to it in the concrete equilibrium of its expression is to see its various component elements in their proper place. How else can we approach the Thomism of St. Thomas himself? Hence, to insist on the overall influence of theological considerations on the form and state of the philosophy in the *Summa*, and to distinguish that influence from the Christian character of the ideas themselves, is to see the thought of St. Thomas in all its concreteness without confusion; indeed it is to see this concreteness exactly as it was by locating each factor in its proper place and seeing the whole in its true perspective.

And this is the point at issue, whether we wish to study St. Thomas as a thirteenth-century figure, or as a guide in our own philosophical work. In both cases we are studying a theologian. That is why to insist on the effects of its theological service on Thomistic philosophy is, by the recognition of their existence, to see the source of these effects in its true place beyond the reach of philosophy and in this way to understand without disfiguring the peculiar ambivalence of a philosophy in ministry to a theology. If Thomism often gives evidence of philosophical incompleteness, this it owes to its theological ministry: St. Thomas developed questions, not as a philosopher, but with the liberty and the aim of a theologian. If we do not notice this theological state and dedication of Thomistic philosophy—by which I mean, specifically, the philosophy in St. Thomas' own writings—then we are in danger of absorbing its theological ministry within philosophy itself, of thereby disfiguring that philosophy by misconceiving it relations to theology, and ultimately of misunderstanding the creative role of that theology in the realm of philosophical ideas. St. Thomas offers the modern reader a philosophy that is both Christian and engaged in theology. To call it Christian by reason of its theological engagement is true but not appropriate, while to call it theological by reason of its Christian character is to confuse its nature with its ministry. To deny that the philosophy in the *Summa* is Christian in order to distinguish it from its theological ministry is to deny an obvious fact, namely, that philosophy as an instrument used by St. Thomas the theologian was transformed *as philosophy* in the process. The Christian philosophy of St. Thomas is not reducible to the Greek philosophy that he read in Aristotle, nor can it be equated with the service to which he put philosophy in the interpretation of *sacra doctrina*: the former is Greek and pagan and the latter is beyond the competence of philosophy as such. The Christian philosophy of St. Thomas is a philosophical reality created out of Greek, Jewish and Arabian philosophical materials but transformed by the intelligence and the faith of their author as a preamble to their theological service. It is not a "pure" philosophy, but a Christian one, and, in part, it owes its intellectual depths and penetration as a philosophy to the mind in which it was born. And if, because it was born in the mind of a theologian, we are bound to recognize the intellectual power of his theology, let us also allow that theology the right to exist on its own terms, as a supernatural wisdom pursuing by means of a metaphysical language the mysteries of the Christian revelation.

CHAPTER SIX

Between Philosophy and Theology

VI

❖

AT THIS POINT the historian of medieval philosophy, including the philosophy of St. Thomas, must finally yield the discussion to the philosopher and the theologian. He can urge them to re-examine the cause of Christian philosophy in the light of its origin in medieval theology. He can urge that there is a considerable difference between a religious philosophy and a theological one. Thomism, as a scholastic philosophy, stands at the crossroads of that difference, and the problem of its followers is not to deny its religious character as the price of asserting its proper distinction from theology. The historian can urge that a Christian philosophy is a peculiar reality. Having been born in theology, having acquired the role of speaking much more for God than for man by being the human voice of the theologian, it can live today only in the neighborhood of theology. This is its calling, so long as it remains united to its original purpose. This is also its challenge and its opportunity—if it wishes to be a philosophy in the modern world. For it must today prove that its original service to theology, while fitting it for such a role, did not unfit it to speak also with a human and rational voice among men. Can it do so? It can, but to do so, it must undo its own modern history, and especially the fear that to call itself a Christian philosophy is to surrender its autonomy to theology.

Today that fear is as unjustified in the light of history as it is untenable in the light of theology. A century ago, when scholastics themselves were still operating under the influence of the Cartesian separation of philosophy from theology, it was understandable that they would (and did) deny that philosophy was Christian. Distinct from theology, whose external government kept it from error, philosophy could be only philosophy pure and simple.[1] But today, in principle at least, we are past such a view of scholasticism. The scholastic philosophy of the Middle Ages appears to us, not as the self-contained and monolithic philosophical synthesis cherished by

---

1. The general outlook and occupation of the scholastic thinker of one hundred years ago (including the denial of "Christian philosophy") can be seen from the comments that Constantin Sierp, S.J., wrote by way of introduction to his French translation of Joseph Kleutgen's famous exposition and defense of scholastic philosophy. See C. Sierp, Avant-propos to the translation of J. Kleutgen, *La philosophie scolastique exposée et défendue* (Paris: Gammes Frères et J. Duprey, Editeurs, 1868), I, pp. vii-xvi.

De Wulf, nor as the equally self-contained Thomistic philosophical synthesis espoused by Father Mandonnet, but as the manifold creation of theologians within their theologies. It was theologians who created what has been called an autonomous philosophy. It was theologians who taught us the very distinction between philosophy and theology that we have used so freely against theology in the modern world. Surely, to isolate philosophy from theology by means of a distinction forged by theologians is in some sense to fight a battle where there is no war. We owe medieval theologians the very ideals of philosophical freedom and rationality that we are defending today. It is time that we returned, not so much to those ideals in themselves, since we never abandoned them, but to the mystery surrounding their creation. After playing the sterile game of agreeing with the reason of the rationalist and the unbeliever, after trying for several centuries to defend reason by posing as pure philosophers in the world of the philosophers, today the scholastic philosopher—and especially the Thomist—is in a position to face directly the mystery of a philosophy that was born in a Christian climate and within the world of theology.

That scholasticism was born as a Christian philosophy within theology, recognizable as philosophy in the specificity of its ideas, but nevertheless engaged in a theological ministry, is not an easy idea to grasp. In part, it is not easy because we are used to modern categories—for example, to the view that theology is limited to the realm of mysteries, while philosophy has for its domain naturally knowable truths. We find it difficult to think that theology can generate a philosophy *within* itself as its own human instrument. Such, however, was the theology of St. Thomas Aquinas. In part, too, and for the same reason, we tend to think that philosophy as the *ancilla theologiae* not only defines the nature of scholastic philosophy but also emphasizes its subjection to theology. For, if scholastic philosophy is the handmaid of theology, is it not a servant, an enslaved human reality? Yet it is *in theology* that philosophy is a servant of theology, not in its nature even as a Christian philosophy; and in theology the ministry of philosophy is a higher vocation and for this reason alone a service. Philosophy is a servant only *within* the household of her mistress; she is a servant not of another human science but of that which is divinely revealed truth in theology. What servitude is it to be the servant of God? Such, for St. Thomas, is the ministerial role of philosophy in theology. In the hands of the theologian philosophy is no longer a purely human science; it shares in the divine foundation and mission of his work, and if it contributes the human intelligence and metaphysics for such a work, its role is to let revealed truth articulate itself as much as possible in human form, its role is not to give a philosophical account of mystery. The ministerial role of philosophy within theology is, in fine, a higher mode of life than reason can pretend to; in theology philosophy is a genuine reason, but a religious one, and its rational work consists in letting faith speak through it. Only, to do so defines, not its nature, but its ministry; and that it can do so presupposes a unity of truth between revelation and reason that is one of the deepest marks of the Thomistic theology. Though with infinite inadequacy, the theologian can still try to speak with a human language but in the line of the divine revelation among men because this human world belongs to the same world of truth as does revelation. Both are from God, both are directed at man, both constitute a single providential divine order in which man is living.

If this be true, the ministerial role of philosophy within theology, far from being in any sense a servitude, is the acceptance of its total freedom in the presence of divine truth. The purpose of its ministry is to bring human truth, humanly acquired, to the work of building, under the leadership and the guidance of faith, divine truth in the form of a human edifice—theology. How could philosophy perform such a service within theology unless in principle it could contribute the human wisdom for this edifice? That revelation exists undoubtedly proves the need of a higher light by which men might guide themselves to their end. But that theology exists proves that *philosophia humana* is worthy to share in a divine ministry; when it does, however, it is *sapientia divina* that proceeds *ex principiis philosophiae humanae.*[2]

Once we locate the ministerial role of scholastic philosophy where it belongs, namely, not in itself but in the light of divinely revealed truth, we are in a position to recognize both the nature and the vocation of such a philosophy. It is a Christian philosophy and, as a philosophy, it has a Christian mission. As a philosophy, it is open to the influence of faith, and its vocation is to be, not one more philosophy in the world, but a bridge between philosophy and theology. It is a philosophy engaged in two dialogues, with the philosophers and with the theologians, and it is called upon to live at the boundary between reason and revelation, between pure philosophy and the *doctrina fidei.* To the philosophers its mission is to speak as a Christian philosophy, with an open and genuine acceptance of both the noun and the adjective in its name. It must speak as an engaged philosophy—as truly engaged as are the philosophies of Jaspers and Heidegger, who wish to be nothing but philosophers. To such men it must prove by its philosophical engagement, the authenticity of its effort. It cannot do this by pretending to be a-Christian as a philosophy; it can do this only by working to show, by the evidence of its own reality, that the Christian religion can inspire and promote philosophical

2. St. Thomas, *SCG* II, c. 4, §4.

doctrines, just as it can show on historical grounds that the philosophers have lived rather frequently on religious capital without knowing it.

The dialogue with the philosophers is not an easy one, but scholastics will have taken their first step in this effort when they accept without reservation the principle that seems to have guided St. Thomas Aquinas, namely, that, barring human failings, philosophy and theology can never disagree. Let the modern scholastic philosopher, therefore, commit himself to being fully and without fear a philosopher rather than a philosophical critic; let him also fully and openly acknowledge that there is a religious light at the center of his mind and let him show by his work that the effect of this light is to open his understanding to a deeper awareness of truth. If Heidegger thinks that a Christian philosophy is not possible because philosophy is *inquiry* and the Christian does not inquire, let the Christian in philosophy show that revelation has not replaced philosophy nor does faith substitute for reason. Let him show in detail that when scholasticism flowered in the thirteenth century it was an authentic intellectual inquiry conducted by men who were believers and theologians. It was no less an authentic inquiry for being the work of theologians; on the contrary, its theological service provoked its creativeness. And what scholasticism did once it can do again.

To be sure, the theologian does not need philosophy to establish religious truths since these rest on the authority of God Himself. But he needs philosophy for the sake of men, and for the work of crossing from revelation to their world. His crossing will be as effective in its human communication with men as the philosophy he uses in presenting divine truths to them. Scholasticism was born as such a philosophy, so engaged. Had there been no scholastic theology—a theology speaking the metaphysical language of being—there would have been no scholastic philosophy, and no need of one: there would have been no world beyond philosophy to which philosophy might be open and in whose light it might strengthen its own. Thus, the *Christian* character of scholastic philosophy—and, first and foremost, of Thomism—identifies its nature and reveals its mission. As a philosophy, it has the nature to live only in a world in which nature and reason are engaged in their own way within a higher order of truth that both includes and transcends them. Scholasticism is the sort of philosophy that lives only as a Christian philosophy in a world illumined by faith, in which theologians speak for God with the language of reason in order to draw men to the Christian revelation.

And this is the permanent signature of scholasticism: it can live as a philosophy only if it accepts the truly difficult role of being a philosophy in a world in which there are theologians. It is not a theology and it is not competent to say what its theological ministry might be: this is for the theologian to say. But it can say what philosophical principles are and what they mean: this is for the philosophizing theologian to accept from the philosopher. Let scholasticism, therefore, accept what its historic vocation demands of it all the more in the modern world in which there are philosophers and scientists, and in which there are worlds of knowledge beyond the ken of a medieval theologian. Let scholasticism—and, especially, Thomism—be the intellectual bridge between revelation and philosophy that the theologian must cross in speaking for God to men and that the philosopher himself must finally come to cross in speaking for man on his way to God.

CLUNY MEDIA

Designed by Fiona Cecile Clarke, the Cluny Media *logo depicts a monk at work in the scriptorium, with a cat sitting at his feet.*

The monk represents our mission to emulate the invaluable contributions of the monks of Cluny in preserving the libraries of the West, our strivings to know and love the truth.

The cat at the monk's feet is Pangur Bán, from the eponymous Irish poem of the 9th century. The anonymous poet compares his scholarly pursuit of truth with the cat's happy hunting of mice. The depiction of Pangur Bán is an homage to the work of the monks of Irish monasteries and a sign of the joy we at Cluny take in our trade.

"Messe ocus Pangur Bán,
cechtar nathar fria saindan:
bíth a menmasam fri seilgg,
mu memna céin im saincheirdd."

Printed in Poland
by Amazon Fulfillment
Poland Sp. z o.o., Wrocław

85640043R00067